PLAYING CHORD PROGRESSIONS
ON THE GUITAR IN ANY KEY

By Joff Jones

ISBN 978-0-7935-2750-2

HAL•LEONARD®
CORPORATION

7777 W. BLUEMOUND RD. P.O. BOX 13819 MILWAUKEE, WI 53213

Chord progressions are the backbone of any song...

If you know chord progressions you can...

play any song in any key on guitar!

Everybody knows "the guy that can play anything he knows in any key," not after five minutes of struggling and second guessing, but **right now!** He smiles while he plays because he knows that chord progressions cut right to the heart of any song. And knowing how they behave is an important part of his process. He recognizes them for what they are – short sequences of chords being hooked together to create a longer sequence. Being familiar with these short sequences can put you in the league with... "the guy."

THE TOOLS

Each chord sequence is presented to you in its lowest playable position and can only be played in a **higher** position. By omitting open strings each sequence is movable. The combination of chord grids, music and tab will reassure you that you are "doing it correctly"

The chord grids show what each individual movement looks like.

The music staff shows the chord sequence in a typical rhythmic duration..

The tab staff makes it easier to grasp the routing occurring on the fingerboard.

The Roman numerals at the top of each page are a reference tool - observe but don't get obsessed.

GETTING STARTED

STEP 1 Choose any chord sequence in this book.

STEP 2 Get the sequence in your head to the point that you are thinking of the chord combination as a single entity.

STEP 3 Move anywhere **up** the fingerboard and play the pattern you have just memorized.

STEP 4 **Do not** try to think of what key you're in or roman numeral function.

STEP 5 Just hear it and play it.

APPLYING WHAT YOU'VE LEARNED

STEP 1 Pick up a songbook or fakebook that has chord symbols above the standard notation staff.

STEP 2 Stay away from the songs that you already play.

STEP 3 Dive right into a song that you have never played.

STEP 4 Distill the complex chord symbols into simple ones. If you see an F7♭9 just play F7.

STEP 5 Look for the sequences that you have learned in this book.

THE BIG LEAGUE

STEP 1 Memorize the chord progression in its original key.

STEP 2 Move to a new position on the fingerboard and play the same chord progression in the new key.

STEP 3 Use common fingers when moving to new chords.

STEP 4 Rely on hearing, feeling, with no thinking or calculating.

Tonal Center

I

The tonal center is the place that the chord progression is trying to get to. It can be where you start or where you end up. It seems to maintain a certain presence no matter where in the progression you happen to be. It pulls you toward it. Any of the chord forms shown below can be considered the tonic. However, the dominant 7th is more likely to show up in a blues format.

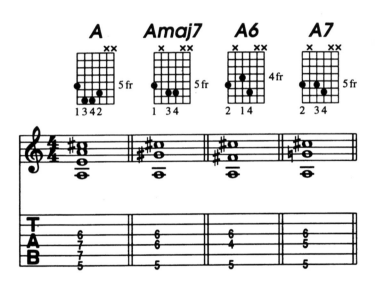

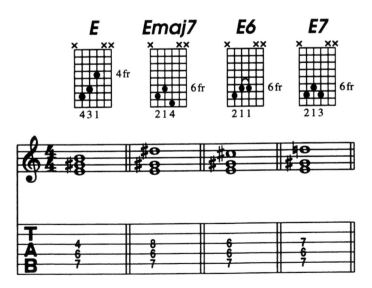

Tonal Center

i

In some instances the tonal center shifts to the relative minor known as vi minor. However, once the chord progression begins to revolve around the vi chord, it becomes difficult to hear and think of it as vi minor. The minor tonality possesses the same basic elements of a major tonality like ii minor and V7. With this in mind, it is easier to hear and think of i minor.

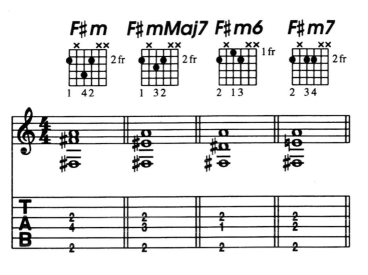

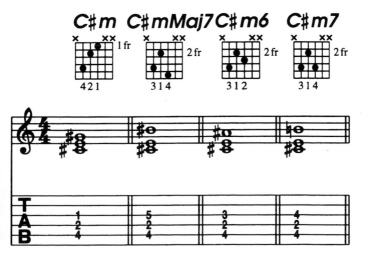

Two - Five

ii V₇

This sequence is the building block of many chord progressions. The 5th degree of the chord, even in its altered state is unnecessary for getting to the heart of a chord progression. The omission of the fifth degree streamlines your chord vocabulary and increases the probability of nailing a chord progression the first time through. Your ultimate goal.

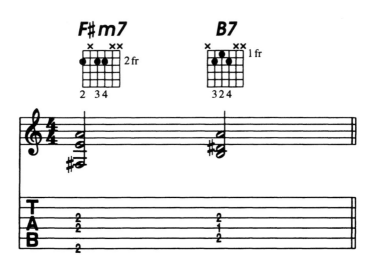

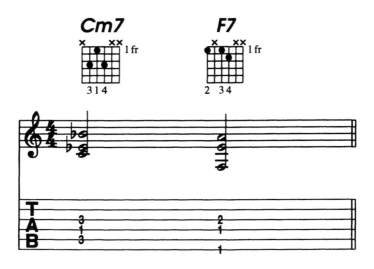

Two - Five
II_7 V_7

This dominant version of a "two - five" has a bolder, even harsher quality. Melody permitting, it is interchangeable with ii - V7.

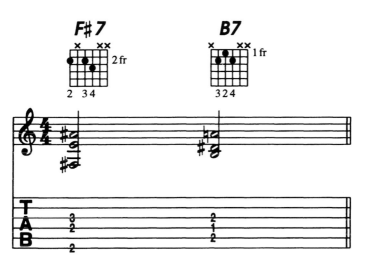

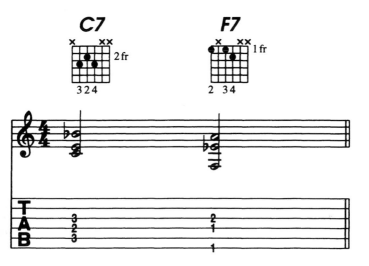

Cycle 5

iii   vi   ii   V₇

This sequence is the diatonic form of "cycle 5" with no alterations. It can be played continuously as a vamp, but the last time through, the V7 will push into the I chord.

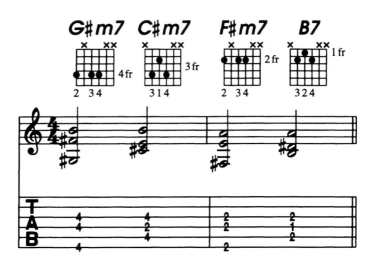

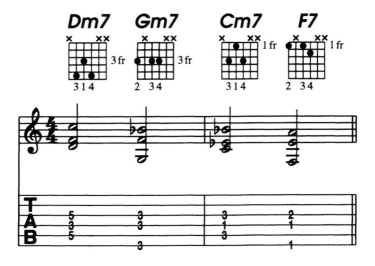

Cycle 5

iii   VI₇   ii   V₇

The "three - six - two - five" sequence is quite flexible in terms of major and minor. The VI7 chord is a slight departure from the diatonic vi minor, but the overall effect of the sequence is the same. The V chord still needs to be a dominant 7th. Reverse the measures to get ii - V7 - iii - VI7. A well known sequence.

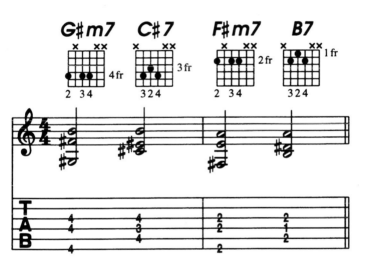

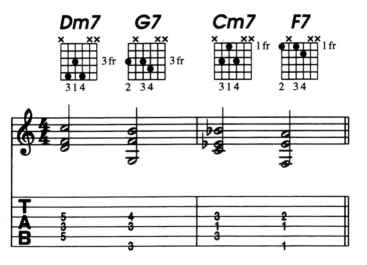

Cycle 5

III₇ VI₇ II₇ V₇

This "cycle 5" sequence is the boldest yet, with all dominant 7ths. When someone plays this, they really mean it.

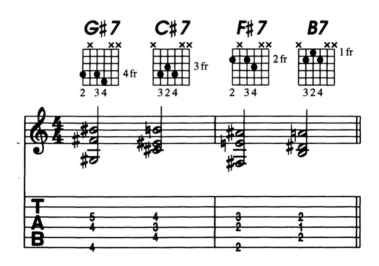

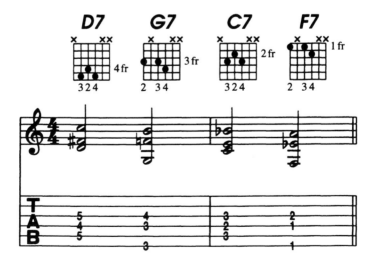

Turnarounds

I   vi   IV   V₇

This turnaround is more basic and obvious sounding. It appears in many songs as the first 2 bars or even the first 4 bars. The IV chord is often replaced by ii minor.

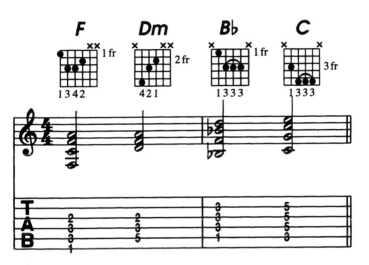

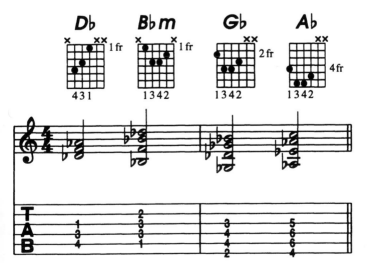

Turnarounds

I   vi   ii   V₇

The purpose of a turnaround is to get you back to the beginning of a tune. Try using this sequence in combination with "three - six - two - five" to build an intro.

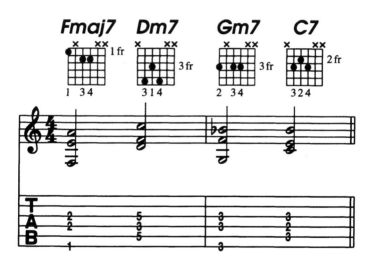

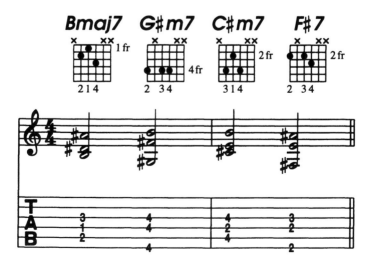

Turnarounds

iii   ♭iii   ii   V₇

This sequence is a "three - six - two - five" in disguise. The ♭iii keeps things moving.

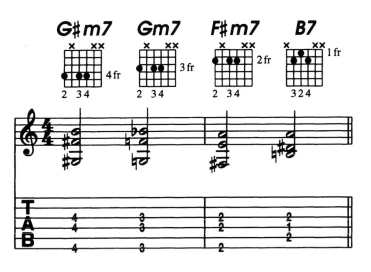

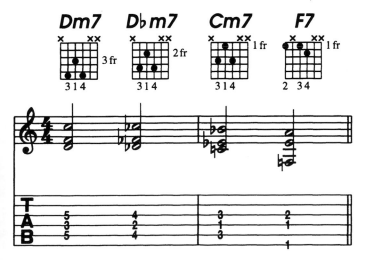

Turnarounds

$i \qquad vi^{\varnothing} \qquad ii^{\varnothing} \qquad V_7$

This minor version of "one-six-two-five" carries a darker sound in a ballad and sounds mischievous at a fast pace.

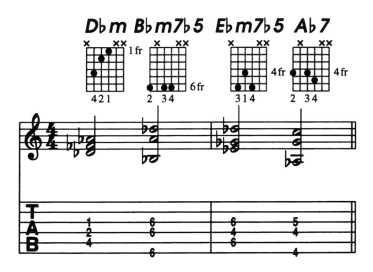

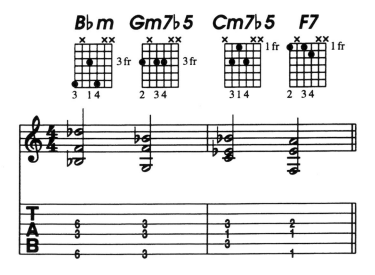

Suspension

I   V₇   I

This is the primary sequence that suspensions are built on. Its purpose is to create motion.

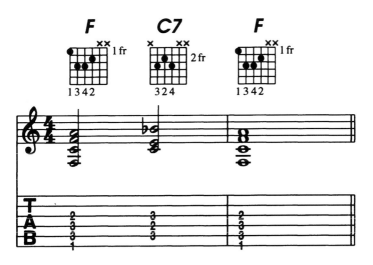

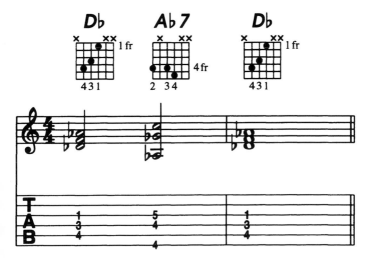

Suspension

$$i \qquad V_7 \qquad i$$

This is the minor counterpart to the previous page. The V7 chord serves the same function in both cases.

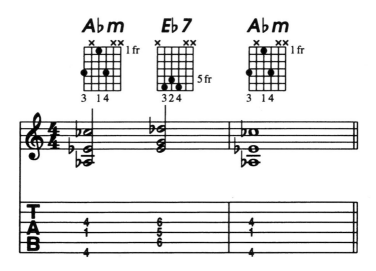

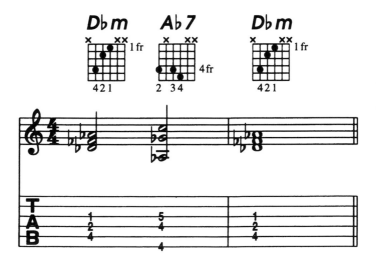

Suspension

i ii° i vii°

The diminished chords in this sequence are really the V7 chord in disguise. Both the ii diminished and the vii diminished want to resolve back to i minor. So, their dominant function is retained.

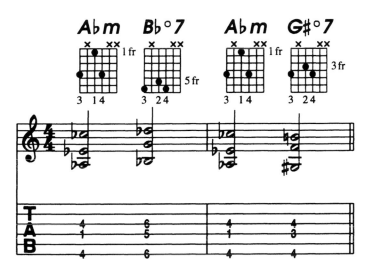

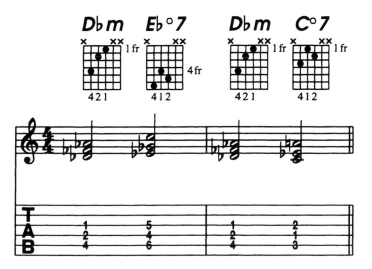

Suspension

I   I°   I

When this sequence is thought of as a whole, the I° diminished is only a slight detour that keeps the I major chord in motion.

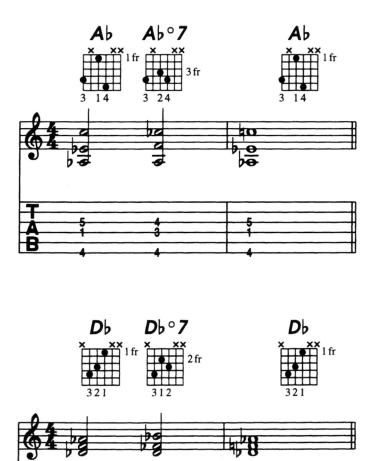

Suspension

$$\text{I} \qquad \flat\text{VII} \qquad \text{I}$$

Major 7th and dominant 7th chords are also quite common in this sequence. Regardless of chord type, the ♭VII chord has the push of a V7 chord.

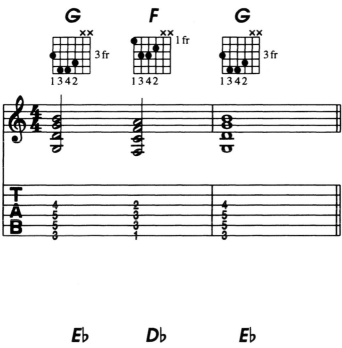

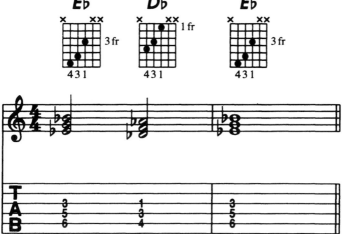

Suspension

Experiment with various 7th chords. The ♭II
pushes back down to I.

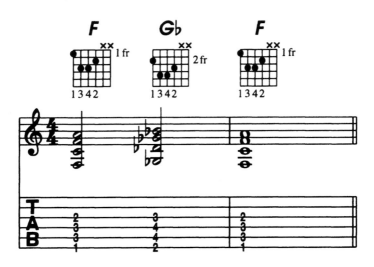

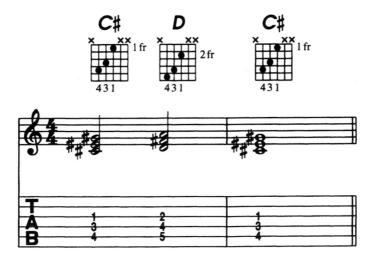

Suspension

I   IV   V

The IV chord easily moves back to I. However, it doesn't quite have the urgency of a V7 chord. Major 7ths and dominant 7ths work well here.

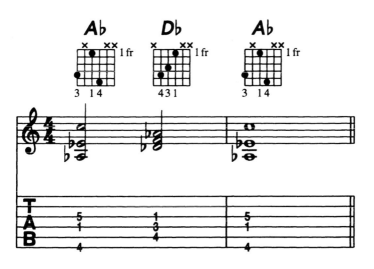

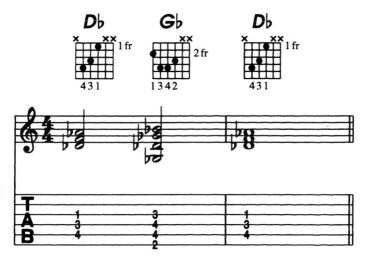

Suspension

i   iv   i

This is the minor counterpart to the previous page. Many times the iv chord contains the 6th degree.

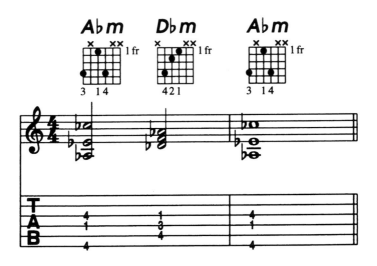

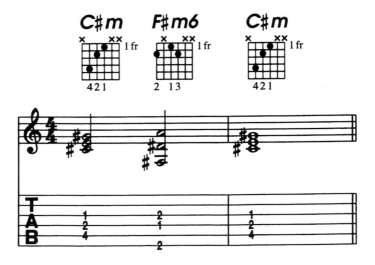

Ascending

I ii iii IV

This sequence sounds extremely diatonic sounding. It is perfectly fine to play them as straight triads. This sequence can also be played in reverse. The IV chord can sometimes be replaced by ii minor for a more circular impression.

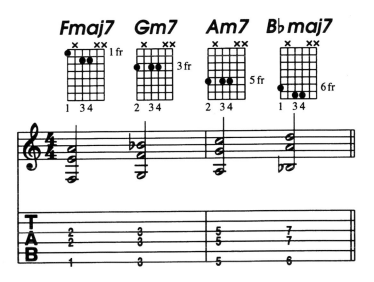

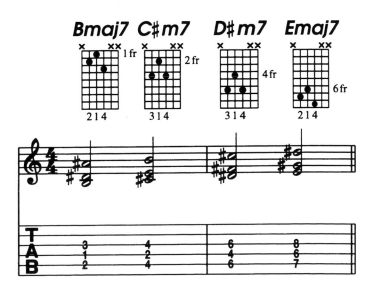

Ascending

$$\text{I} \qquad \text{\#i}^\circ \qquad \text{ii} \qquad \text{\#ii}^\circ$$

This sequence has an ascending "quality," but in reality is a I - VI7 - ii - V7 in disguise. However, it is much more effective to focus on the quality and just play it.

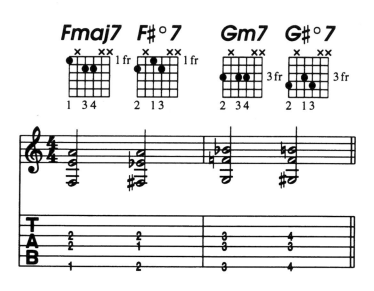

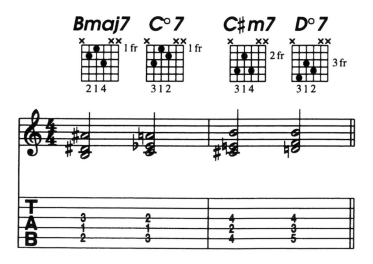

Ascending

I   ii   ♯ii°   I/III

This is an effective filler of space when the I chord is stagnant. It is important to consider the style you are playing in to see if it is appropriate. This sequence has a tendency to overpower the melody and pull the focus away from it.

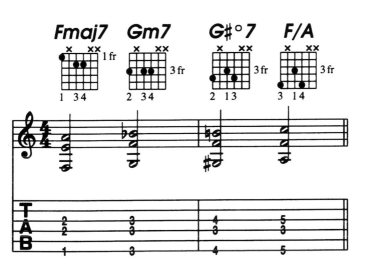

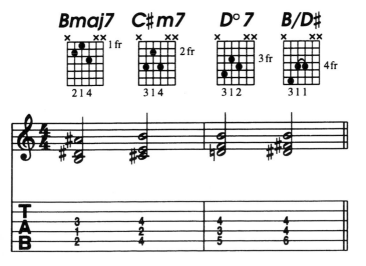

Ascending

ii   iii   IV   V$_7$

Notice the physical distance covered in the examples below. This sequence could be re-routed to cover less ground, but playing this way helps you to think in a more linear fashion.

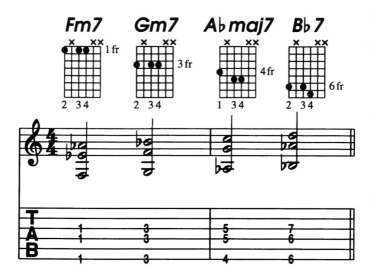

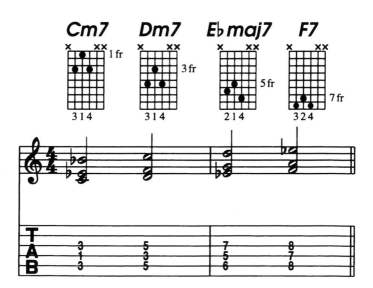

Descending

In the bottom example, the minor tone in the second chord is heard, even though it is not being played.

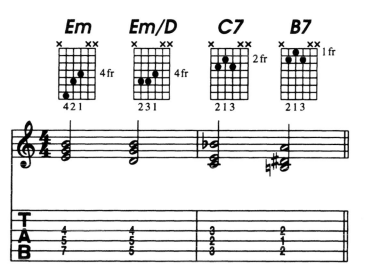

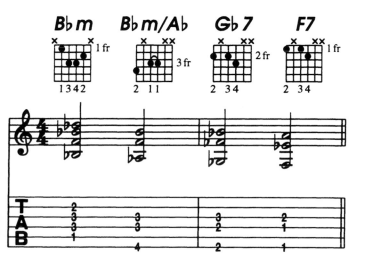

Descending

I₇ VII₇ ♭VII₇ VI₇

The fingering for these dominant 7ths are probably not your first choice - until now. They are specifically designed so that you are coiled and ready to strike at the next set of chords. The logical destination for this sequence is ii - V7 - I.

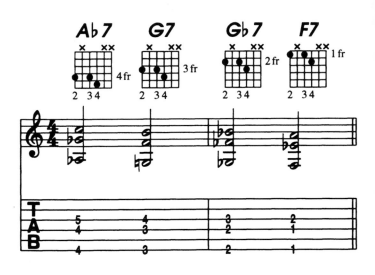

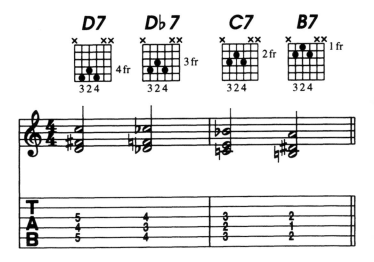

Descending

I/III   ♭iii°   ii   V₇

The root motion gives this sequence its descending quality. In the end, what you actually hear is going to dominate over analyzation.

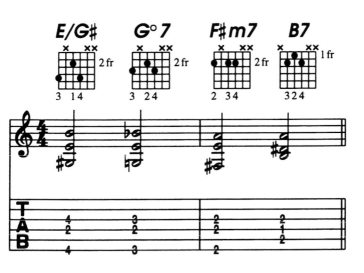

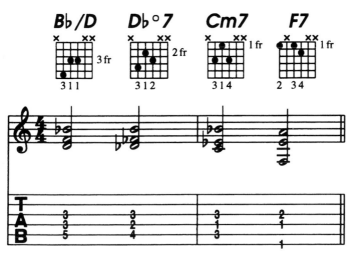

Descending

$\flat\text{iii}$ $\flat\text{VI}_7$ ii I_7

This sequence is a ii - V7 being approached
from above by a half-step. It is also common
for the reverse situation to occur: ii - V7
moving up one half - step away from itself.

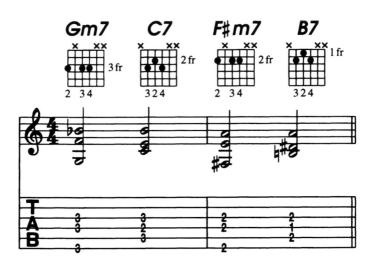

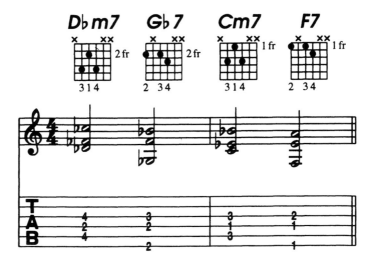

Descending

#iv   iv   iii   ♭iii

After you play the top example, go back through it, omitting the 2nd string. Even though you have removed the altered tones you can still hear their presence in the sequence. The fifth degree is missing from the chord forms in the bottom example, but they can still be imagined.

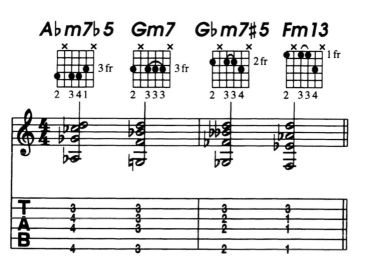

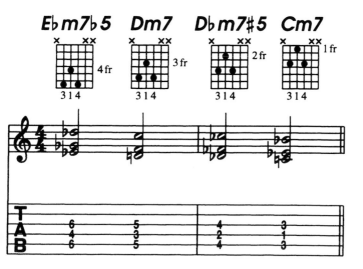

Descending

The ♭5 is an optional tone in this particular sequence. However, all of the minor 7th chords could contain ♭5.

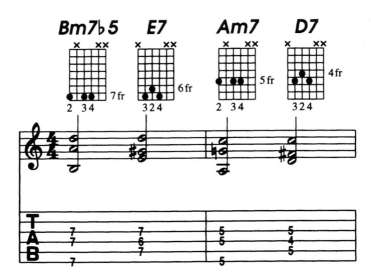

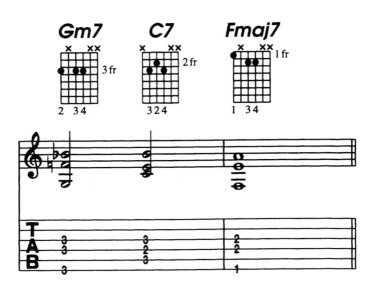

Descending

#iv	VII₇	iii	VI₇
ii	V₇	I	

This example seems long, but is a likely sequence of ii - V7 occurring in "cycle 5."

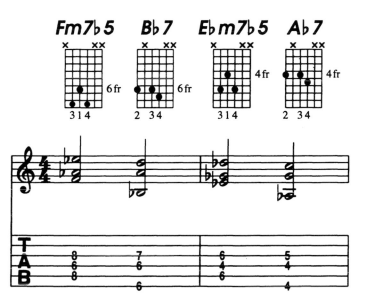

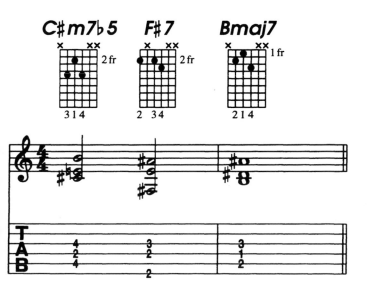

Line Clichés

Imaj7   I6

Line cliches have the ability to keep things moving when they are otherwise stagnant. This simple sequence is also a common occurrence on the IV chord.

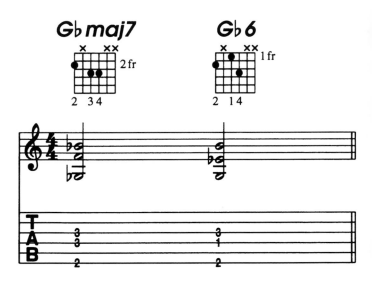

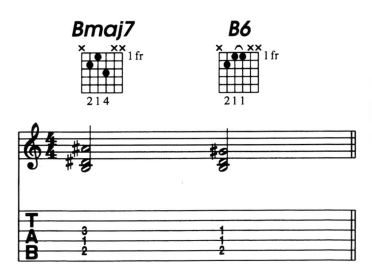

Line Clichés

ImMaj7   Im6

This is the minor counterpart to the previous page. This sequence could easily appear as the iv minor chord.

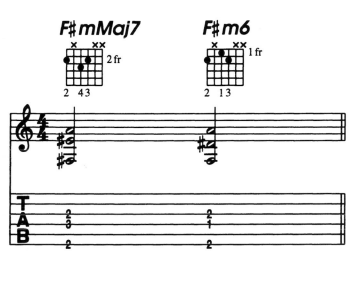

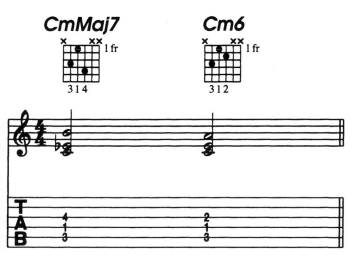

Line Clichés

I   Imaj7   I7

This sequence has a tendency to move to the IV chord, as the I chord is transformed to a dominant 7th.

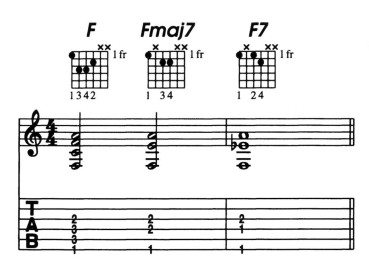

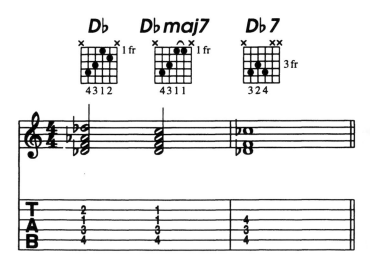

Line Clichés

Im ImMaj7 Im7 Im6

This sequence is used to create motion while at the same time establishing a minor tonal center.

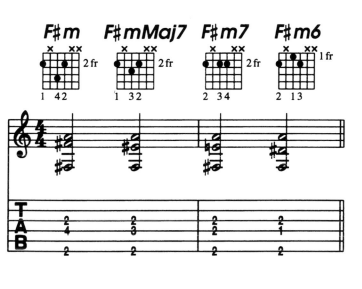

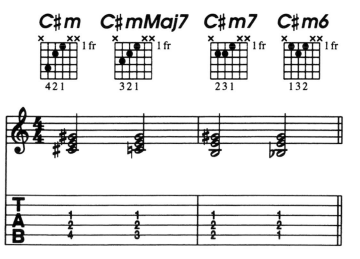

Line Clichés

I   I+   I6

The fingerings below are designed to help
you get where you are going next. The
direction of this sequence can continue up to
the ♭7th degree or back down to +5.

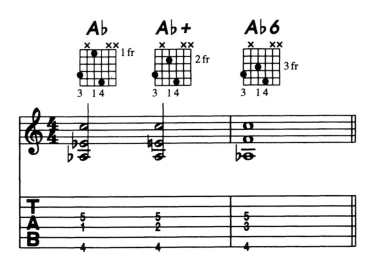

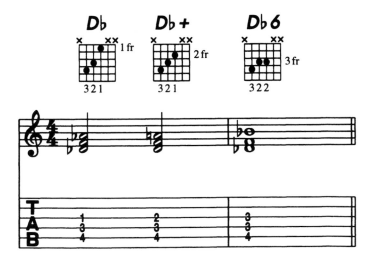

Line Clichés

Im   Im+5   Im6

This is the minor counterpart to the previous page. It carries the same flexibility of moving upward or back down. This sequence can simply come to rest on the 6th degree.

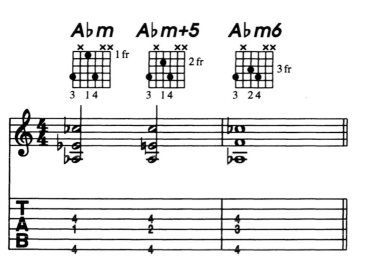

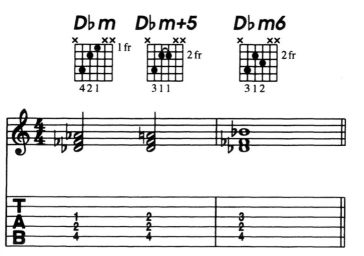

Pivotal

$$I \quad v \quad I_7$$

This sequence is a common preparation for
moving to the IV chord at the bridge of a
tune. The v minor creates motion, but it is
entirely possible for I major7 to move directly
to I dominant7. The v - I7 can be thought of
as a "two - five" in the new key.

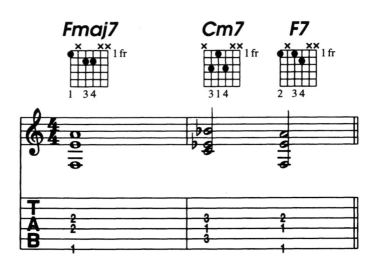

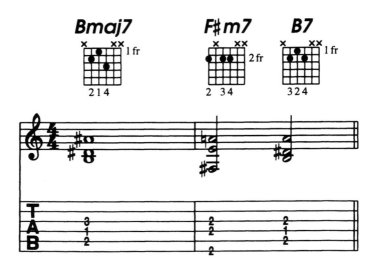

Pivotal

$$\text{I} \qquad \flat\text{V}_7 \qquad \text{VII}_7$$

This sequence is a likely preparation for shifting from the original key into a new key up a major 3rd.

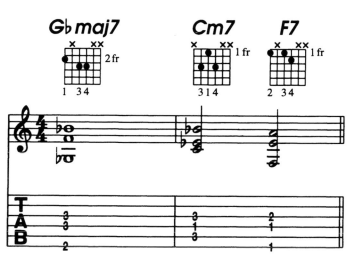

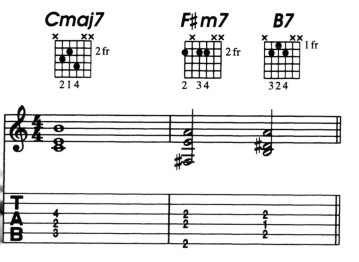

Pivotal

I   vii   III₇

This sequence shifts into the major key a minor 3rd down from the original. For a smooth shift into the relative minor, it is common to see the ♭5 contained in the vii chord. It is still not necessary to include that tone in your chord voicing to outline the chord progression.

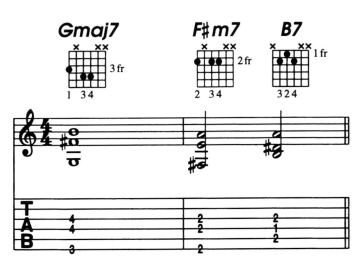

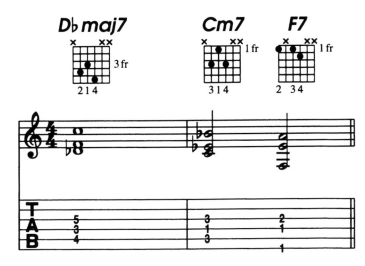

Pivotal

I   ♯i   ♯IV₇

The ♭ii - ♭V7 is really ii - V7 in the new key one half - step down from the original. For a shift to a minor key, the ♭5 is a common occurrence in the minor 7th chord.

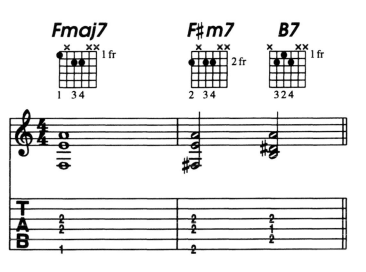

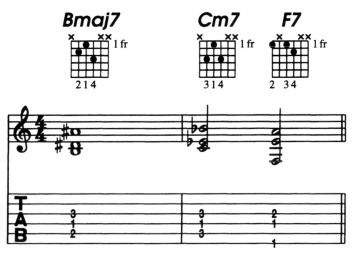

Pivotal

I　　　　　**♭vii**　　　**♭III₇**

This preparation will land you in the key a major 3rd down from the original. As before, the ii - V7 is your ticket. When you see a minor chord followed by a dominant 7th chord see if it can be thought of as a "two - five".

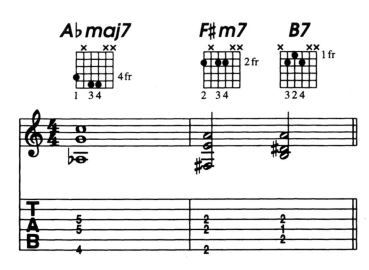

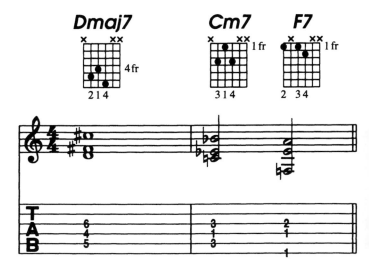

Pivotal

$$II_7 \qquad\qquad ii \qquad\qquad V_7$$

This culprit is responsible for many chord progressions gone wrong when being played for the first time. The II7 moving to ii minor gives the illusion that you are in "cycle 5." The tendency is to go one chord beyond what you want. In "cycle 5" that's pretty far away.

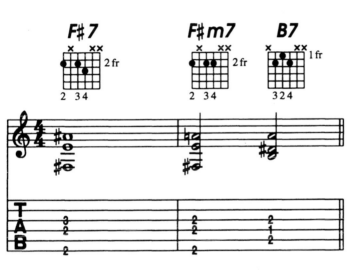

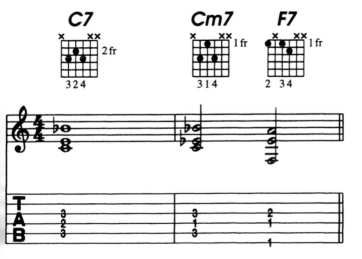

Pivotal

I   ♭V₇

The tendency of the bV7 is to push down into
the IV chord. In a diatonic chord progression,
this slight detour adds a nice lift. This
sequence is a combination of "far out" mixed
with predictability.

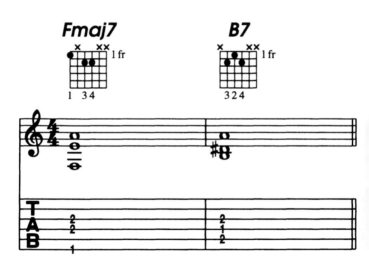

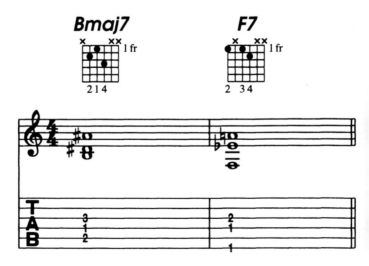

Pivotal

ii   iv   ♭VII₇

The iv - ♭VII7 is a ii - V7 in the new key, up a
minor 3rd from the original key.

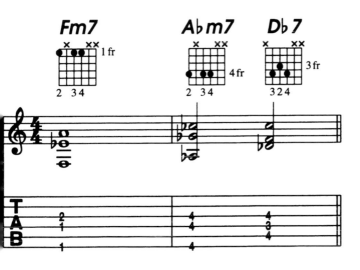

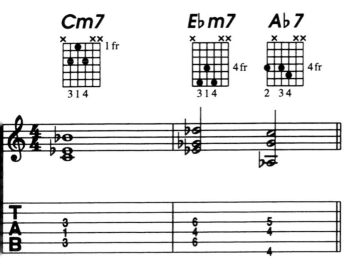

Pivotal

vi   VI₇

This small adjustment from minor to major gives the VI chord more clout. The natural tendency from here is for "cycle 5" to go into effect with ii - V7 - I.

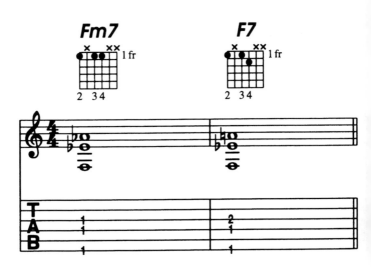

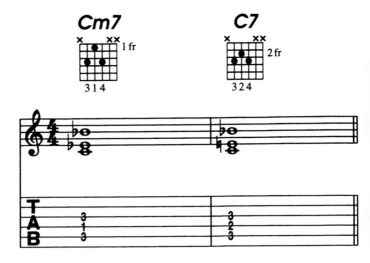